Calling All Angels

A Guide to
Communing with Angels
for Personal and
Planetary Assistance

by
Christine Chalenor

with Visionary Art by
Cheryl Yambrach Rose

Dedicated to my family. I love you all more than you could ever know. Each one of you is such a precious gift to my soul. Thank you for all your loving support.
Love, Christine

© Copyright 2001
by Christine Chalenor
All rights reserved

Printed in Korea

ISBN: 0-9700902-2-6

Published by:

**Mt. Shasta Light Publishing
P. O. Box 1509
Mt. Shasta, CA 96067-1509 USA**

Phone: 530.926.4599
Fax: 530.926.4159

Email: aurelia@mslpublishing.com

Website: www.mslpublishing.com

Contents

Part 1: Communicating with Angels--
Past and Present --------------------------- 9
My First Angel Experience -------------------- 11
Angelic Visitations for Everyone -------------- 17

Part 2: Communicating with Angels--
from the Essene Tradition ---------------- 25
Introduction to the Sacred Covenant ----------- 27
The Sacred Covenant ------------------------- 32
Communions --------------------------------- 37

Morning Communions ---------------------- 39
Morning Prayer ------------------------------ 41
Saturday Morning Communion
   Sabbath with the Earthly Mother ----------- 43
Sunday Morning Communion
   with the Angel of Earth -------------------- 44
Monday Morning Communion
   with the Angel of Life --------------------- 45
Tuesday Morning Communion
   with the Angel of Joy ---------------------- 46

Wednesday Morning Communion
  with the Angel of Sun ---------------------- 47
Thursday Morning Communion
  with the Angel of Water ------------------ 49
Friday Morning Communion
  with the Angel of Air --------------------- 50

Evening Communions --------------------- 53
Friday Evening Communion
  with the Heavenly Father ----------------- 55
Saturday Evening Communion
  with the Angel of Eternal Life ------------- 56
Sunday Evening Communion
  with the Angel of Creative Work ---------- 57
Monday Evening Communion
  with the Angel of Peace ------------------ 58
Tuesday Evening Communion
  with the Angel of Power ----------------- 59
Wednesday Evening Communion
  with the Angel of Love ------------------- 60
Thursday Evening Communion
  with the Angel of Wisdom --------------- 61

Part 3: Communicating with Angels--
Prayers for the World ---------------------- 63
Personal Prayers ---------------------------- 65
The New Millennium Prayer ------------------- 68
Prayer to Father/Mother God ----------------- 71
Daily Attunement ---------------------------- 72
The Meal Blessing --------------------------- 74
Divine Abundance ---------------------------- 76
Prayer for Compassion ----------------------- 78
Divine Direction ---------------------------- 80
Prayer for Love ----------------------------- 82
Rekindle the Flame of Love ------------------ 85
Personal Protection ------------------------- 87
Earth Protection Prayer --------------------- 88
Protection While You Sleep ------------------ 90

Prayers for Healing ------------------------ 93
Healing Prayer 1 ---------------------------- 96
Healing Prayer 2 ---------------------------- 98
Healing Personal Conflict ------------------- 100
Healing Conflict with My Mother ------------- 102
Healing Conflict with My Father ------------- 104
Healing a Personal Violation ---------------- 106

Children's Prayers ------------------------- 111
The Youth of the World --------------------- 113
Prayer for the Youth of the World ---------- 114
Children's Daily Prayer --------------------- 116
Children's Prayer to Release Anger ---------- 118
Children's Prayer to Release
   Sadness --------------------------------- 120
Children's Nightly Prayer ------------------- 122

Summary -------------------------------------- 123
About the Visionary Artist ------------------ 125
About the Author ---------------------------- 126
Contact and Ordering Info ------------------- 127

Visionary Art
by Cheryl Yambrach Rose

1. The Third Pillar --------------------------- 8
2. Earth Rapture ----------------------------- 16
3. Merlin Awaits ----------------------------- 24
4. Mary in the Stellar Wheel ----------------- 36
5. Iona -------------------------------------- 42
6. Fairy Glen -------------------------------- 48
7. Divine Transmutation --------------------- 52
8. Archangel Michael ------------------------ 62
9. Tristan and Isolde ------------------------ 84
10. Angel of Truth --------------------------- 92
11. Wings ---------------------------------- 110

Part 1

Communicating with Angels – Past and Present

My First Angelic Experience

The first memory I have of an Angel was also my first meeting with Jesus. I was around two-and-a-half years old. I remember it very clearly, and years of study have given me the language to describe it. My older brother, who was not yet four years old, had almost suffocated while playing with a plastic bag. Our mother had been so upset she cried. She explained how we could die if we didn't breathe and that the plastic bag had stopped my brother from being able to breathe.

As I laid in bed that night I started to think about my breath. I became worried that I would forget to breathe if I fell asleep. After I did fall asleep, I soon awoke with a huge gasp. I was now sure I had forgotten to breathe, so I focused very intently on my breath. In and out it went. I followed it through my lungs. I felt it going into my feet. It filled my head and arms. It seemed to be everywhere. Over and over I breathed in and out, again and again.

Something strange began to happen to me. My body felt as if it were growing larger and getting very heavy, but at the same time I was getting smaller somewhere deep inside. Then I remember a pop. Everything in my third dimensional reality just disappeared. I was a single flashing pinion of light. I saw only millions of flashing and blinking lights.

At this point I became very frightened. Then a memory suddenly came to me: when I had been baptized, at around fifteen months old, the minister had asked me if I wanted to take Jesus as my personal savior. As I looked at him blankly, the minister explained that Jesus would be my comforter, and if I were ever afraid I could call to Jesus and He would take that fear away. I remember smiling and thinking that was a good idea, as the minister then drew the sign of the cross with holy water on my forehead and mumbled some more words.

As I recalled this, realizing I was now in fear, I began calling out, "Jesus come, Jesus come, Jesus come." Over, and over, and over, I repeated those two words in my mind. I don't know how long I repeated them, but it seemed like a very long time. Then just as I had been promised, He appeared.

I could see Jesus very clearly amidst all the sparkles of light. As He looked at me with His soft smile, He seemed so familiar, as if I had known Him forever. The fear that had gripped me began to subside as a warm feeling started in my very center and moved slowly outward replacing any trace of fear. Encircled in a bubble of warm, comforting love, I found myself instantly back in my bedroom with Jesus.

He began to talk with me. He said, "You don't ever have to be afraid. You have a guardian Angel who watches over you." He told me my Angel could protect me from all harm. Jesus then told me to look up above my head. I looked up; there standing behind the head of my bed, smiling down at me, was a beautiful Angel. He told me to remember my Angel and that He and the Angel were always there for me. He also said to call if I ever needed either of them. Jesus then talked with me for some time. I drifted off to sleep, feeling warm and comfortable, rocked in my own personal Angel's arms.

This was the beginning of a lifelong personal relationship with Jesus, my guardian Angel, and over time many other Angels.

Based on my personal experience and years of study, I believe in my heart that Angels are real; they are all around us, all the time. You, too, can communicate with them and develop a personal relationship. You can use the communions and prayers in this book as a beginning point. Then create your own prayers for the issues you face in your everyday life.

I started this book with just one prayer, the Prayer for the Youth of the World. After creating that prayer, other prayers started flowing in, filling my thoughts and dreams. I was often awakened in the wee hours of the morning as a new prayer came flooding in. I learned to keep a pen and pad next to my bed.

My hope is to inspire you to commune with the Angels and with God, be it the Father and/or the Mother aspect, and grow more into that spiritual Being we all long to be, with a greater appreciation for this beautiful Planet and the great gift of life.

Angelic Visitations for Everyone

"Angel" means messenger. We know Angels as intermediaries between earthly and heavenly worlds, powerful and yet gentle. With their radiant light, overwhelming beauty, and glorious wings, they are a reassuring presence that brings comfort, insight, at times miraculous healing, and always the promise of eternal life.

Angels are manifestations of a God who chooses not to show Himself directly. Angels are most often represented in human form; that is, transfigured with brilliant light and supernatural attributes. Different aspects of God are often associated with different Angels. Gabriel is the divine messenger. Michael protects and defends the faithful. Raphael brings healing and truth. Chamuel is the Angel of love, art and beauty. Jophiel imparts wisdom. In the Essene religion the Angels are referred to by their attributes alone:

The Angel of Power, The Angel of Wisdom, The Angel of Life, The Angel of Water, The Angel of Air, and so on.

In ancient religions like those of Egypt or Greece, the line between gods and Angels was a thin one. In that time we had lesser gods; they went to God on our behalf. Each divine attribute was seen as separate and given an individual title. Some were seen as having wings, all having the ability to help those who asked. This sounds very similar to the Angels as described by the Essenes. However, these gods had human emotions and you were at their mercy. All were free to pray to these deities for assistance and blessings.

Christianity and Islam made a much stronger distinction, teaching to pray only to God, "the one true God". If you repented and were pious He would send you help. This would most likely be from his Angels, but only a chosen few were worthy of receiving a message from God through one of these holy creatures.

Those who professed to have visions or messages from Angels were usually condemned, and often killed.

Angels have been artistically depicted in many different religions and cultures. We find Angels in classical mythology and philosophy, in shamanistic visions, in Zoroastrianism, Hinduism, Buddhism, Taoism, and ancient Egypt.

In more modern times, we have been given a great deal of information. For instance, we have the works of Madam Blavatski, the founder of the Theosophical Society. She gave amazing accounts of visitations from Angels and other divine beings. She had psychic gifts from the time she was a small child, and these were her firsthand accounts. She also gave considerable information on these beings, their purpose, and how to commune with them.

Alice Bailey also gave very detailed information on Angels, the higher realms where they lived, and the importance of prayer.

Guy W. Ballard wrote many books corroborating both these women's information. He also brought through direct messages which he called dictations from many different Angels and other divine beings from these higher realms.

Many different teachers of our own times receive messages, write books, and teach classes on the subject of Angels.

Dr. Edmond Bordeaux Székely gave us *The Essene Gospel of Peace* and many books that followed, filled with the original Essene teachings and information on Angels and communion with them.

Elizabeth Prophet and her organization, the Teachings of the Ascended Masters, wrote many books with information on Angels and she also gave instructions and conveyed the importance of prayer and communing with the Angels.

J.J. Hurtak wrote *The Keys of Enoch* and *The 72 Names of God;* both give fabulous insights into Angels and the mysteries of the higher realms. Hurtak imparted the importance of chanting or singing the sacred names of God, some of which are Angels.

Patricia Cota-Robles, Barbara Marciniak, Norma Milanovich, Joshua David Stone, and many others continue to write books on these blessed beings and the different ways they assist mankind. All of these very gifted people receive their information firsthand. They all reiterate the importance for each of us to commune with the Angels.

I have devoted Part 2 of this book to the Essene teaching on Angels. When I first read this information I could feel my soul leap with excitement. Part 2 begins with the Sacred Covenant, the original text Moses received from God. This text clearly indicates that God always intended for us to commune with the Angels. In the Sacred Covenant we find God's specific instructions on how, when, and why to commune with the Heavenly Father, the Earthly Mother, and their Angels.

Following the Sacred Covenant are the Essene daily Communions. This knowledge of prayer to the Angels was given to the dedicated Essene only after several years of daily meditation. These are the actual Communions the early Essenes repeated every morning and evening. I have copied them from the original transcriptions by Dr. Edmond Bordeaux Székely, with special permission by Swallow Székely. I am so very grateful for this work and the gift to use it here. I highly recommend all of his books (see page 127 for ordering information).

In Part 3 are prayers invoking the Angels and asking for their assistance with the varied issues and challenges of our lives. Angels work in a very high vibration of love. To commune with them, center yourself and contemplate love. Even if you are praying because you are afraid, sad or in some kind of pain, you still must come from the place of love to make the connection.

Some people think they can command an Angel to harm someone. Angels exist in the higher realms of pure unconditional love. Anger, hate, fear, pain, and lower vibrations don't exist there. The person asking for such a thing is only sending his own energy out to do harm.

Angels would never harm anyone. Energy moves in a circle. Whatever you send out will eventually come back to you. Remember karma; you reap what you sow. As a child my inner guidance was constantly reminding me of the Golden Rule: do unto others what you would have them do unto you. It still helps me today when I find my emotions starting to kick in. So send out loving, good, and kind thoughts and prayers, and the Angels will be able to help you and bestow many blessings.

Part 2

Communicating with Angels – from the Essene Tradition

Introduction to the Sacred Covenant

The oldest and one of the richest sources of information I have found on communication with Angels is *The Essene Gospel of Peace*. This is a series of books which were translated by Dr. Edmund Bordeaux Székely. He worked from the *Dead Sea Scrolls and* ancient manuscripts in Aramaic and old Slavonic that he found through years of painstaking research in the secret archives of the Vatican and in the Royal Library of the Habsburgs now held by the Austrian government.

The Sacred Covenant is contained in *The Essene Gospel of Peace, Book 2.* In this incredible text, God tells us who He is and how to seek Him out. He impels us to make a special time to study his Laws, to commune daily with the Heavenly Father, the Earthly Mother, and their

Angels, telling us that as these Communions evolve, so will our understanding of ourselves, God, and the universe. God gives us explicit directions on communing with certain Angels at very specific days and times. He tells us that by using the communions we will find Him and the Laws of the Universe, and ultimately immortality.

This Sacred Covenant is ancient. Moses directly received it and all the information it contains from God Himself. It was inscribed on the two tablets that Moses received on Mount Sinai and later broke. When he returned to the mountain to speak with God again, God told him to keep those original commandments in his heart and teach them to others who were ready to receive them. These would be the Sacred Covenant between God and the Children of Light.

For the masses who had not yet dedicated their lives to God, He then gave Moses a new set of commandments, the

Ten Commandments that most of us were taught as children

Moses himself kept the Sacred Covenant and taught it to the Elect in the Essene Brotherhood, those who chose the path of light by dedicating their lives to God and His Laws. Before receiving the information on actually praying to the Angels, the aspirant had to complete several years of contemplation on the various Angels and their specific attributes each morning and evening. This gave the disciple the time to raise his energy to the level of Love the Angels work in.

Jesus was an Essene and his original teachings include communing with the Heavenly Father, the Earthly Mother, and their Angels.

In the Essene Communions, on each day two different Angels are invoked, one in the morning and one in the evening, except the Sabbath. The Sabbath starts at dusk Friday night and goes until dusk on Saturday. On Friday evening the

Communion is with the Heavenly Father and on Saturday morning the Communion is with the Earthly Mother.

The Angels called in the mornings are explained to be Angels of the Earthly Mother. These Communions are given when you first wake up. Those communed with in the evenings are the Angels of the Heavenly Father. You ask these Angels to teach you through the night as your body sleeps.

Following each of the Communions I have included a brief visualization. This was an important part of the practice in this early teaching.

Before beginning the morning Communions, there is a prayer to be given when you first wake up, which I call the Morning Prayer.

The Earthly Mother, or Earth Mother, is what we know as Mother Nature, a beautiful, powerful, feminine being whose sole job is orchestrating this third-dimensional reality. Her Angels are the directors of the Elements: Earth, Air, Fire, Water, Life and Joy.

From this incredible information found in the Sacred Covenant and the Communions, it is evident to me that God always intended for us to commune with these Angels. The instruction for this has been around for a very long time, as we have seen. Once reserved for only those considered to be worthy, **communication with the Angels is now available to all who feel impelled towards it.**

Since we live under the Law of Free Will, the Angels are not allowed to help us unless we ask. So ask!

Go pray with them! You can pray for Nature, for your family and loved ones, for others, and for any situation. Discover how prayer with the Angels can change your life. Many blessings await you!

On the following page is the portion of the Sacred Covenant that relates to prayer with Angels.

The Sacred Covenant

Honor thy Earthly Mother,
that thy days may be long upon the land.
Honor thy Heavenly Father,
that eternal life be thine in the heavens.
For the earth and the heavens are given
unto thee by the Law, which is thy God.

Thou shalt greet thy Earthly Mother
on the morning of the Sabbath.
Thou shalt greet the Angel of Earth
on the second morning.
Thou shalt greet the Angel of Life
on the third morning.
Thou shalt greet the Angel of Joy
on the fourth morning.
Thou shalt greet the Angel of Sun
on the fifth morning.
Thou shalt greet the Angel of Water
on the sixth morning.
Thou shalt greet the Angel of Air
on the seventh morning.

All these Angels of the Earthly Mother
shalt thou greet,
and consecrate thyself to them,
that thou mayest enter the
Infinite Garden,
where stands the Tree of Life.

Thou shalt worship thy Heavenly Father
on the evening of the Sabbath.
Thou shalt commune with the
Angel of Eternal Life
on the second evening.
Thou shalt commune with the
Angel of Work on the third evening.
Thou shalt commune with the
Angel of Peace on the fourth evening.
Thou shalt commune with the
Angel of Power on the fifth evening.
Thou shalt commune with the
Angel of Love on the sixth evening.
Thou shalt commune with the
Angel of Wisdom on the seventh
evening.

All these Angels of the Heavenly Father
shalt thou commune with,
that thy soul may bathe in the
Fountain of Light,
and into the Sea of Eternity.

The seventh day is the Sabbath:
Thou shalt remember it, and keep it holy.
The Sabbath is the day of the
Light of the Law, thy God.
In it thou shalt not do any work,
but search the Light,
the Kingdom of thy God,
and all things shall be given unto thee.
For know ye that during six days
thou shalt work with the Angels,
but the seventh day shalt thou dwell
in the Light of thy Lord,
who is the Holy Law.

A Guide to Communing with Angels

Communions with the Heavenly Father, the Earthly Mother, and Their Angels

The weekly repetition of each of these communions, depending on your dedication, ability, and consistency, will allow you to absorb, use, and direct these currents of energy for your own evolution, mankind, and the planet.

Morning Communions

Morning Prayer

*To be said every morning
when you first awaken.*

In reverence
to the path of Light,
I enter the eternal and infinite
garden of mystery,
my spirit in oneness with
the Heavenly Father,
my body in oneness with
the Earthly Mother,
my heart in harmony with
my Brothers,
the sons of men.

Saturday Morning Communion
Sabbath with the Earthly Mother

Morning Prayer: (see page 41)

The Earthly Mother and I are one.
Her breath is my breath;
her blood is my blood;
her bone, her flesh, her bowels,
her eyes and ears,
are my bone, my flesh, my bowels,
my eyes and ears.
Never will I desert her.
Always will she nourish
and sustain my body.

Contemplation:

Feel the power of the Earthly Mother flowing through your body like a mighty river swollen with rains, rushing and roaring with a great noise.

Sunday Morning Communion with the Angel of Earth

Morning Prayer: (see page 41)

*Angel of Earth,
Awaken the regenerative energies in me.
With your power give new life
to my whole body.*

Contemplation:

Imagine the Angel of Earth flowing through the earth, energizing every seed to sprout, bringing new life. This same Angel brings life to your whole body. Feel every atom, cell, and electron being completely regenerated.

Monday Morning Communion with the Angel of Life

<u>Morning Prayer</u>: (see page 41)

*Angel of Life,
With your power enter my limbs
and give strength to my whole body.*

<u>Contemplation</u>:

Imagine the Tree of Life as a great oak; see yourself embrace it. Feel the power of the Angel of Life flow to your arms, to your legs, and to all the parts of your body, as the sap flows in the tree in the spring. So will the Angel of Life fill you with the ecstasy of the Earthly Mother, the power of Life.

Tuesday Morning Communion with the Angel of Joy

Morning Prayer: (see page 41)

*Angel of Joy,
Descend upon earth and fill me,
mankind, and all beings with your
beauty, delight and happiness.*

Contemplation:

Imagine the Angel of Joy painting the sky, the flowers, trees, and grasses; filling all nature with beauty. Breathe in the sweet scents of the flowers. Listen with new ears to the songs of the birds. See with new eyes the colors of the sunset.

All these things will cause joy to well up inside you. Let the joy and beauty fill your heart.

Wednesday Morning Communion with the Angel of Sun

<u>Morning Prayer</u>: (see page 41)

*Angel of Sun,
Enter my body
and let me bathe in the fire of life.*

<u>Contemplation</u>:

Feel the warmth and radiation of the sun filling your solar plexus and the center of your body just below your navel. See it radiating out in all directions, filling your whole body with golden light.

So warm. So wise. So compassionate.

Thursday Morning Communion with the Angel of Water

Morning Prayer: (see page 41)

*Angel of Water,
Enter my blood;
Give the Water of life
to my whole body.*

Contemplation:

Imagine the rain washing the whole earth clean; see it becoming a stream. Feel the Angel of Water as the currents of this stream send the power of the Earthly Mother through your blood, cleansing, healing and purifying your entire body.

The power of the Angel of Water is very great.

Friday Morning Communion with the Angel of Air

Morning Prayer: (see page 41)

Angel of Air,
Enter with my breath.
Fill all my lungs,
and give the Air of Life to my body.

Contemplation:

Concentrate on your breath. Feel only your breath as you rhythmically inhale and exhale. Feel yourself floating in the sky, light as a feather, filled with the Angel of Air, rising closer and closer to the Heavens.

The Angel of Air is the messenger of the Heavenly Father.

Evening Communions

Friday Evening Communion with the Heavenly Father

(Beginning of Sabbath)

As you close your eyes to sleep say:

The Heavenly Father and I are one.

<u>Contemplation</u>:

Close your eyes and imagine yourself held in the great arms of the Father, soaring to the unknown realms of Heaven, bathed in the light of the stars. With His touch springs a fountain of knowledge, love, wisdom, power and the splendor of eternal light.

One day the eyes of your spirit shall open and you shall know all things.

Saturday Evening Communion with the Angel of Eternal Life

As you close your eyes to sleep say:

*Angel of Eternal Life,
Descend upon me and give
Eternal Life to my spirit.*

<u>Contemplation</u>:

Imagine the oneness of all life. Let your spirit soar up beyond the earth. See with the eyes of spirit golden threads linking you to all life everywhere, and to that which is Eternal.

Sunday Evening Communion with the Angel of Creative Work

As you close your eyes to sleep say:

*Angel of Creative Work,
Descend upon me and all humanity,
giving abundance to me
and all the sons of men.*

Contemplation:

Imagine the whole planet working together like a hive of bees, all giving their service for the whole in harmony. As you work, so will this most powerful Angel of the Father, the Angel of Creative Work, nurture and ripen the seed of your spirit, that you may see God.

Monday Evening Communion with the Angel of Peace

As you close your eyes to sleep say:

> *Peace, peace, peace,*
> *Angel of Peace,*
> *Be always everywhere.*

Contemplation:

Follow the golden streams of light, the garment of the Angel of Peace. Peace is the key to all knowledge, all mystery, all life. Seek it out in all that lives. Seek it in the family, humanity, culture, and with nature. Imagine the world living in peace.

Bring back to the morning the Peace of God.

Tuesday Evening Communion with the Angel of Power

As you close your eyes to sleep say:

*Angel of Power,
Descend upon me.
Fill with power and the will of God
all my deeds.*

<u>Contemplation</u>:

Imagine yourself floating in the Heavens, fully charged and empowered by the stars, realigning yourself with your divine purpose, with divine power that is the will and strength to succeed, and the energy to bring it into fruition.

Wednesday Evening Communion with the Angel of Love

As you close your eyes to sleep say:

Angel of Love,
Descend on me.
Fill with love all my emotions.

<u>Contemplation:</u>

Imagine yourself floating on a large lake filled with holy water, charged with divine unconditional Love, soothing all your emotions, absorbing into your very cells pure Love. See it beaming out from you to all people everywhere.

Kind deeds and gentle words come from a heart bathed in Love.

Love is eternal.

Thursday Evening Communion with the Angel of Wisdom

As you close your eyes to sleep say:

*Angel of Wisdom,
Descend upon me.
Fill with wisdom all my thoughts.*

<u>Contemplation</u>:

Imagine your thoughts as powerful as a bolt of lightning severing the stormy sky. See the golden light of wisdom purifying these thoughts. Let the Angel of Wisdom guide you to use wisdom in all you think, say, and do.

Only with Wisdom will order and harmony govern your life, allowing the unknown realms to be revealed.

Part 3

Communicating with Angels – Prayers for the World

Personal Prayers

Here are a few prayers using the different principles I have learned from my years of study and my love of communication with God and the Angels.

These prayers are written in hopes that anyone from any religious background can open this book and feel comfortable saying them. It might be appropriate for you to change a word or two here or there for a prayer to apply to your particular situation or spiritual belief. Please feel free to do so. These prayers are for you.

You will see that as each prayer starts, it has an invocation calling to God, and then to the Angels. I left out God as Mother because for so many this is a new concept. If you are ready to include the Mother aspect of God in these prayers feel free to do so. Where the invocation starts with Heavenly Father, add "and Earthly

Mother," and where the invocation starts with God you can say "Father/Mother God."

Each time you call to the Angels you bring your consciousness closer to their realms, opening the path of communication and creating a specific momentum, making it easier each time, until the energetic flow between you and the Angels is like a mighty stream of light permeating your entire being and world and the worlds of all those you come into contact with.

So, dear ones, pray without ceasing, until the prayers fill your mind, conscious and subconscious, and your dreams, so that a prayer is always dancing on the tip of your tongue and you are ready in a moment to whisper or shout from the roof top the prayer to solve the issue at hand. This is just a beginning.

I like to start out or end my prayers with an intimate conversation with these dear Angels, thanking them for their presence in my life, the changes I have experienced, and all the gifts I perceive to be in correlation to my communication with them, etc. . . .

Let these prayers calling to the Angels guide you to a wonderful new world filled with prayer, Angels, and a new-found closeness to God.

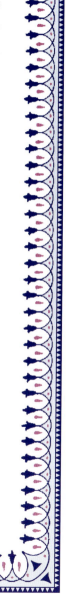

The New Millennium Prayer

Beloved Heavenly Father,
Beloved Earth Mother,
Source of All Life,
and Great Angelic Hosts,
hear our prayer
for the New Millennium.

Let humanity come together
and embrace this time
of great awakening,
together creating
a collective intention
to restore ourselves and our planet
to the highest potential,
that we may live in a world of peace.

Help us develop
the spiritual courage and strength
to positively greet this time
of great change and transition
with faith and trust.

May we stand firm in our knowing
that our future will become
what we envision and choose to create.

As we awaken from our long sleep
to embark on this inward journey,
hold us in your loving embrace.

Guide our focus from money,
power, and material possessions,
to the love, joy, and gentleness
of the spirit within.

Heal us from all wounds
and negativity,
as we allow the grace
and compassion of forgiveness
to abide within,
washing away all resistance to change.

For in this moment we choose love,
compassion, joy, healing,
forgiveness, understanding,
tenderness, wisdom, and peace.

Let us embody the courage
to live in divine truth,
acknowledging the constant victories
in every day.

Thank you, Dear Ones,
for all you have done to create
this wonderful planet
and these incredible bodies,
the beauty of nature, depth of emotions,
the intricate and vast sensation
of all the senses,
so great and glorious a gift.

We look forward in sweet anticipation to
what awaits us
in this New Millennium.

We embrace you in our heart of hearts
until once again we can be joined
in the sacred oneness.
And so it is.

Amen, Amen, Amen

Prayer to Father/Mother God

Beloved Heavenly Father
and Earthly Mother,
I take refuge in the idea of you,
ever-present, all powerful, all knowing,
directing and creating all that I see,
all that sustains me, all that I am.
My past, my present, my future,
every blink of my eye, beat of my heart,
and stirring emotion,
every atom, cell and electron
within this form,
so complex, so diverse
is your great gift to my soul.
Give me the wisdom to live with honor,
humility, compassion, and grace.

Oh God, you are so magnificent.
I Am, I Am, I Am adoring Thee.
And so it is.

Amen

Daily Attunement

Dear God,
Send your glorious Angels
from every aspect of the Divine,
the Archangels, Seraphim,
Cherubim, and the Elohim,
to set me in perfect alignment
and balance.

Beloved Angels of God,
I call for perfect alignment:
my spirit with the Heavenly Father,
my body with the Earthly Mother,
my heart with humanity.

Beloved Angels of God,
seal my aura in the purest white light,
filling me with clarity and purpose.
Encircle this with ultraviolet light,
deflecting all discord;
that I stay balanced and grounded
in love, wisdom, and power.

Beloved Angels of God,
stay with me the next 24 hours,
guiding and illuminating with
wisdom and divine intellect.
Let all tasks flow with ease and joy,
brilliantly completed,
manifesting ample abundance.

Beloved Angels of God,
hold the immaculate concept for me,
for perfect health and balance
in all aspects of my body.
Maintain and strengthen the divine
blueprint for my life stream.

Beloved Angels of God,
let me walk in humility,
with compassion and tenderness
in my regard for nature
and all mankind.
So be it.

Amen

The Meal Blessing

Beloved Heavenly Father
and Earthly Mother,
all Angels and Elementals
who together have provided
such a glorious bounty
to nourish and sustain us,
we appreciate these great gifts.
We now call for the blessing
of all gathered here.

(Pause to feel the blessing.)

We call for the blessing of this food.

(Pause again.)

Charge it with your great light.
Charge it with your perfect love.
Purify and perfect it in every way,
transmuting any imbalance
or negative aspects,
reestablishing its highest
nutritional value.

We send love, appreciation,
and blessings
to all hands who helped in any way
to bring these gifts to our table.
Send this blessing all the way back
to the sun, the wind, the rain,
and the earth.

Thank you God. (3x)
So be it.
And so it is.

Amen

Divine Abundance

Beloved Heavenly Father,
Send your glorious Angels,
from every aspect of the Divine,
to assist me in creating
prosperity in my life.

Beloved Angels of God,
I call forth my divine abundance.
Shower me with the gifts,
attributes, talents, and powers
stored in the realms of light,
from my own good works
and God's grace.

Beloved Angels of God,
I open myself now to receive.
I resonate with prosperity
and self worth,
aligned with wisdom
and compassion.

Beloved Angels of God,
all belief and attachment to lack
or limitation dissolves forever
in the light of the Law.
I am filled with your pure love
and truth of source.

Beloved Angels of God,
I accept prosperity and abundance
in its myriad forms,
with grace, ease, and humility.
Thank you for your great service.

And so it is!

Amen, Amen, Amen

Prayer for Compassion

Beloved Heavenly Father,
Send your Angels of Compassion
to fill me with your great compassion.

Beloved Angels of God,
I open myself to receive
divine compassion now.

As this compassion fills me,
I am consumed by unconditional love.
All judgment, criticism and prejudices
dissolve completely.

Beloved Angels of God, soften my heart.
Let it beat with constant compassion
and understanding.

As this compassion fills me,
I am free from all negativity,
as feelings of tenderness and grace
resonate now within.

Beloved Angels of God,
Let me regard all with
your great compassion,
finding dignity and beauty
in diversity.

And so it is.

Amen

Divine Direction

Beloved Heavenly Father,
Send your glorious Angels of Wisdom,
Direction, and Creative Works,
to assist me to find my divine purpose.

Beloved Angels of God,
send divine direction my way.
Guide me to my perfect work.
By thy Love I pray.

Celebrate my soul's reunion
with the blueprint of my life.
Expand throughout my consciousness
your qualities of light.

Liberate and develop my own
individual talents,
aligned to my highest potential,
in humility,
with harmony and balance.
Let your great light now

enfold all my soul,
to guide me and help me,
at last, reach my goal.

Beloved Angels of God,
send divine direction my way.
Guide me to my perfect work.
By thy Love I pray.

Thank You God.

So be it and so it is.

Amen

Prayer for Love

Dear God,
Send your Divine Angels of Love
to nurture my heart,
and realign me with pure, true,
unconditional love.

As a rose unfolding fair
wafts her fragrance through the air,
let it stir the pure emotion,
perfect Love from the cosmic ocean.

Let that Love all through me flow,
feeling oneness and purity grow,
till the whole earth is a
glowing pink sphere,
radiating love pure and clear.

Angels of Love,
envelop my soul.
Purify my heart and make me whole.

I am filled with the fire of Love,
resonating with God above.
Into the earth it flows from me,
setting all nature and life now free.

Angels of Love,
envelop my soul.
Purify my heart and make me whole.

Up from the earth comes
the reciprocation,
eliminating all sense of separation.
I Am aligned with God above,
the earth and man all one in Love.

As a rose unfolding fair
wafts her fragrance through the air,
let it stir the pure emotion,
perfect Love from the cosmic ocean.

So Be It. (3x)
And So It Is.

Amen

Rekindle the Flame of Love in my Marriage

Beloved Heavenly Father,
Send your great Angels of Love,
to bless the sacred union of my marriage,
and rekindle the flame of Love.

Beloved Angels of Love,
Destiny brought us together;
let divine Love keep it so.
Strengthen this union to grow
more and more in Love each day.
Bridge any opposition that may come.

Beloved Angels of Love,
In times of disagreement and frustration,
fill us with patience,
understanding, and peace;
our emotions flowing harmoniously
as our souls swim the ever-changing
sea of life together.

Beloved Angels of Love,
When some may falter or doubt,
and look elsewhere,
direct our focus towards each other,
that we find comfort held
in familiar arms of Love,
again seeing that reflection of God.

Beloved Angels of Love,
Let the sound of his/her voice
still quicken my heart.
May I find joy in his/her gentle touch
and relaxation in the refuge
of his/her presence.

Beloved Angels of Love,
Rekindle the flame of Love between us,
that this marriage be victorious,
as we walk the path towards God
together aglow in Love.
So be it.

Amen

Personal Protection

Beloved Heavenly Father,
Send Archangel Michael
and his legions of blue lightning
Angels of power, protection,
and the will of God,
for divine protection, here and now!

Archangel Michael,
Seal me in your sphere of light,
*Angels
before me, behind me,
to the right, to the left,
above, and below,
encircled in love and protection
wherever I go.

And so it is.

Amen

*(3x, 9x, 12x or more)

Earth Protection Prayer

Beloved Heavenly Father,
Creator of all things
in Heaven and earth,
Protect my life, my family, my world.

Through your great love,
wisdom, power, and mercy,
send your Angels to guard us
from all wars and rumors of wars.

Through your great love,
wisdom, power, and mercy,
send your Angels to guard us
from all cataclysm
and rumors of cataclysm.

Through your great Love,
wisdom, power, and mercy,
send your Angels to transmute
all negative and harmful thought forms,
cause, core, record, and memory.

Through your great Love,
wisdom, power, and mercy,
send your Angels to replace it all
with peace, harmony, wisdom,
healing, and Love.

Through your great Love,
wisdom, power, and mercy,
send your Angels to protect and seal
the earth and all mankind
in your divine will
and divine plan for our future.

I consciously accept this here and now.
Thank you God.
So Be It.
And so it is.

Amen

Protection While You Sleep

Beloved Heavenly Father,
Send Archangel Michael
and your protecting Angels
to guard my body, my home,
and my family as we sleep.

Dear Angels,
Encircle this property,
sealing the corners,
the four directions,
above and below,
with your glorious protecting might.

Fill this home with legions of Angels.
Saturate each one here
with your sacred fire.

Dear Angels,
Guide us in our dreams
high into the Heavens,
sailing through the stars,

to be taught the higher concepts
of wisdom,
that we may know and effectively
follow the Light of the Law,
the path of Light.

Dear Angels,
Help each one of us
to retain this inner knowledge,
lighting a candle of understanding
in each and every heart.

Dear Angels,
Let this protection,
direction, and guidance
go out to all my family of light
across the whole planet.
Let it nurture each and every
precious flame.

So Be It,
And So It Is.

Amen

Prayers for Healing

Healing is for far more than the sicknesses and injuries that affect the physical body. Healing is pertinent for the balancing of all the bodies: the emotional, mental, spiritual, and then the physical. Many of us have experienced a less than desirable childhood. Some have endured severe trauma and even child abuse, and many have lived in dysfunctional families and/or foster homes lacking love and much-deserved nurturing. These sad conditions produce shallow and wounded adults who fear commitment and relationships and are unable to recognize, give, or receive love in its fullest. Instead, they create codependent relationships and repeat the undesirable patterns of their past.

Some of us have experienced personal violations such as rape, incest, physical and verbal abuse, prejudice, and other assaults, all of which can cause severe mental and emotional trauma patterns and scarring.

Here are some prayers to help you

heal, along with the physical body, that wounded inner child and mental or emotional issues that may be blocking inner growth and health. Give way to a new balanced emotional approach to relationships, replacing self-judgment and self-doubt with self-esteem, understanding, and the ability to love yourself and others.

Healing Prayer 1

Beloved Heavenly Father,
Send your Healing Angels
to radiate healing energy on me,
mankind, and all the earth.

Radiant Healing Angels,
I am bathed in your healing light.
Let it penetrate to my very core,
healing, blessing, and strengthening.
I open wide the door,
atoms, cells, electrons,
within this form of mine.
Let Heaven's own perfection
make me now divine.

Radiant Healing Angels,
Move into action to mend the flaws,
completely transmuting
any imperfections,
according to God's Laws.

Radiant Healing Angels,
Regenerate, reformat, and
activate all DNA,
reestablishing the divine blueprint
of my soul,
vibrant life in me reborn,
to heal and make me whole.

Radiant Healing Angels,
I am bathed in your healing light,
miraculously transforming,
held in your glorious wings so bright.
Atoms, cells, electrons,
within this form of mine,
let Heaven's own perfection
make me Now divine.
I accept my healing. (3x)

So Be It and So It Is.

Amen

Healing Prayer 2

Beloved Heavenly Father,
Send your glorious Healing Angels
to shower healing energy on me,
mankind, and all the earth.

Beloved Healing Angels,
I ask for healing for the whole earth,
and all life forms evolving here.
May all sickness, pain, and suffering
dissolve forever.

Beloved Healing Angels,
Shower us with your glorious
healing light,
that we may live in a world
of peace and harmony,
in vibrant good health and strength,
fulfilling our divine purposes.

Beloved Healing Angels,
Step into the aura of each individual now,

continuously realigning each one
to his divine matrix,
until all aspects resonate
and hold this matrix firmly.

Beloved Healing Angels,
Our bodies sway to the melody
of your great presence,
as we bask in your
glorious Healing Light.
Blazing like a Sun,
regenerated and made whole,
our perfect healing is now won.

So Be it, and So It Is.

Amen

Healing Personal Conflict

Beloved Heavenly Father,
Send your glorious Angels of Peace
to help resolve the conflict
between _____.

Beloved Angels of Peace,
Restore harmony, diplomacy, and order
where there has been discord.

Beloved Angels of Peace,
Send compassion flooding from above,
to fill us with patience, tolerance,
understanding, and love.

Beloved Angels of Peace,
Let your golden waves of peace
dissolve all conflict,
judgment, and anger,
erasing all errors,
breaking down all barriers.

Beloved Angels of Peace,
Through your great love
and compassion,
let us find a harmonious solution,
following your golden strands
of light,
to walk again the path of peace.
So Be It!

Amen

Healing Conflict with My Mother

Beloved Heavenly Father,
Creator of all things
in Heaven and on earth,
Send me your Angels
who radiate the love, compassion,
and nurturing energies of the Mother.

Beloved Angels,
Dissolve forever
the emptiness I feel inside
from unresolved conflict
with my mother.
Wrap your glorious wings around me,
radiating love and healing out
in all directions.
Penetrate my mind,
my body,
my emotions,
and my soul,

filling me with the true nurturing,
compassion, and understanding love
of the Mother.

I affirm healing and resolution
on all issues with my mother now.
I open my heart to allow
the love God intended
between mother and child to fill me,
transforming all emptiness into light,
allowing my mind to understand
nurturing love,
freeing my emotions from
fear of rejection,
enabling my heart to give
and receive love,
opening the door for my soul
to move forward
on the initiatic ladder of life.
So Be It!
Thank you God.

Amen

Healing Conflict with My Father

Beloved Heavenly Father,
Creator of all things in
Heaven and on earth,
Send me your Angels who radiate
the love, power, understanding,
and protecting energies of the Father.

Beloved Angels,
Dissolve forever
the emptiness I feel inside
from unresolved conflict
with my father.
Wrap your glorious wings around me,
radiating love and healing out
in all directions.
Penetrate my mind,
my body,
my emotions,
and my soul,

filling me with the true, strong, safe,
and understanding love of the Father.

I affirm healing and resolution
on all issues with my father now.
I open my heart to allow
the love God intended
between father and child to fill me,
transforming all emptiness into light,
allowing my mind to understand
sheltering, protective, supportive
fatherly love,
freeing my emotions from
fear of rejection,
enabling my heart to give
and receive love,
opening the door for my soul
to move forward
on the initiatic ladder of life.
So Be It!
Thank you God.

Amen

Healing a Personal Violation

Beloved Heavenly Father,
Shelter me with your great strength.
Send your Angels of Healing,
Compassion, and Forgiveness
to help me heal this
traumatic violation.

Beloved Angels of God,
Remind me of the inner strength
that can overcome and find wisdom
from every situation.

Beloved Angels of God,
My pain is so deep I feel it hide,
lurking in the dark void
where my innocence did once abide.
Touch it with your magic presence
so I can bring it out and let it go.

Beloved Angels of God,
My heart has closed, I weep in silence,
I find fear where I once felt secure.
Touch this fear with your
great compassion,
that my tears may cease
and I can feel safe once more.

Beloved Angels of God,
Heal the scars in my memory.
Release my dreams from
the agony of recall.
Touch my mind with your
healing and grace,
that I may send these visions
away forever.

Beloved Angels of God,
Shatter the limiting
crystallization of blame.
Let me forgive all.
Touch this judgment with your
wisdom and purification,
that I may once again be understanding.

Beloved Angels of God,
Let revenge, resentment,
and sorrow dissolve,
letting go of attachment
to anger and hate.
Touch my heart,
that I may once again
be compassionate.
So Be It.

Amen

Children's Prayers

The Youth of the World

Our youth need your prayers now, more than ever before. The energies of this world are hard, heavy and desperate. The cases of drug abuse, alcoholism, unwanted pregnancy, depression, despair, teen suicide, anger and violence are skyrocketing.

Please join me, and parents, families and friends around the world, to give this prayer for these sweet souls. We brought them here, so together let us pray for a safer, kinder, more loving environment for them to grow in.

They are our future!

Prayer for the Youth of the World

Beloved Heavenly Father,
Beloved Heavenly Father,
Beloved Heavenly Father,
Take command of our youth today.
Send your Angels now we pray,
the Archangels, Seraphim,
Cherubim, and Elohim
from every aspect of the divine,
to love, heal, illumine, protect,
and bless the youth of the world.

Open their spiritual awareness
and keep them constant to the light,
that they may live their lives
in perfect alignment
to their highest potential,
in harmony with Joy, Peace, Love,
Health, Abundance, Freedom,
Wisdom, and Power.

Bestow your grace and forgiveness
to transmute the inherent sins
of the past.

Nurture the flame of holy innocence
within them,
that they may know their own
personal victory,
and light the path home for all.

So be it, and so it is.

Amen

Children's Daily Prayer

Dear God,
Send your bright Angels
to guide, protect,
and fill me with Love.

Dear Angels, bright Angels,
When I close my eyes,
my thoughts rise to thee.
In silence and wonder
your beauty I see.

Dear Angels, bright Angels,
Remind me of the Golden Rule.
Teach me to be kind,
friendly, and thoughtful.

Dear Angels, bright Angels,
Stay and protect me
and my family all day.
At home, at school,
and when I play.

A Guide to Communing with Angels

Dear Angels, bright Angels,
Fill me with love
from my head to my toes.
Let it bless others wherever I go.

Thank you, dear Angels, bright Angels
now hovering above,
for guiding, protecting,
and sending your love.

Amen

Children's Prayer to Release Anger

Dear God,
Send your great Angels
of Peace and Happiness,
to help me let all anger
and hurt feelings
turn into gentleness and joy.

I had an angry moment,
hurting deep inside,
wanting to be right,
feeling angry pride.

Angels of Peace,
Take this anger away.
I choose to be happy; I like to play.

It hurts to be angry,
your face in a frown,
feeling like others are letting you down.

Angels of Peace,
Take this anger away.
I choose to be happy; I like to play.

I stomped my feet hard,
shook my fist in the air,
roared like a lion,
growled like a bear.

Angels of Peace,
Take this anger away.
I choose to be happy; I like to play.

Look at my face, can you see?
Yes—a grin.
Thank you, dear Angels,
I feel happy again.

Angels of Peace,
Encircle me round.
I'm no longer angry.
My happiness I have found.

Amen

Children's Prayer to Release Sadness

Dear God,
Send your great Angels
of Joy and Happiness,
to help me let all sad feelings
turn into laughter and joy.

When people say
mean things to me,
I feel sad and rejected,
wanting to run far away.

Angels of Joy,
Take this sadness away.
I choose to be happy; I like to play.

When I'm sad,
I just want to hide;
I feel tired, dark,
and empty inside.

Angels of Joy,
Take this sadness away.
I choose to be happy; I like to play.

Down from the heavens
and out from the sun,
I am surrounded by
Angels and Fairies,
glee, giggles, and fun.

Angels of Joy,
Encircle me round.
No longer sad feelings;
my joy I have found!

Amen

Children's Nightly Prayer

Dear God,
Send your great Angels
to protect me, my family,
and my home, as I sleep.

Have them guide my dreams
and the memory to keep.
Let me dream of long ago,
of Kings and Queens of castles tall,
of sunny days and fairies small,
of being happy, feeling love,
and sailing through
the stars above.

When I awake, ready to play,
send your Angels of the day.

Amen

Summary

From a lifetime of study I have come to the conclusion that most religions are basically very similar. They all pray to the same God, although they have different names for Him. Their intentions and goals are also basically the same: to seek out truth, become the best person one is capable of being, have God be pleased with who you have become, and then, ultimately, be granted eternal life in paradise. The differences are mainly in traditions, rituals, ceremonies, and styles of prayer.

We can all grow and flourish together, embracing our similarities and our differences. The point is acceptance—unity in diversity. God created us to be very different from each other. We can honor and enjoy the beauty in this individuality.

Prayer with the Angels is universal; it is for everyone. The Laws of God are there for all who choose to seek. The information you receive will be up to your abilities, in the timing that is appropriate for you, and determined by your intention, capacity of love and consistency.

I love the ancient Essene teaching because it is the most profound I have found concerning actual direct instruction on communion with Angels. My desire is to open your eyes and heart to a new form of prayer to the Angels, who have been here since the beginning of time, just waiting in the wings for you to ask for their help. Cosmic law prohibits them from interfering with your free will. Only if you ask can they then assist you.

> Let the Angels guide
> and help you every day
> as you climb the initiatic
> ladder of light back to God.

About the Visionary Artist

Beginning as a portrait painter, Cheryl Yambrach Rose's painting career has been long and varied. She paints in "parables," images and meanings perceived both by the conscious and subconscious mind. She terms this work "Art through the Eyes of the Soul."

Accompanying Sacred journeys to Britain and Europe, along with the alpine peaks of her home in Mt. Shasta, California, have provided the inspiration and visions for her paintings.

She paints in oil on linen in a studio built according to the Sacred geometry on the ancient Celtic foundation pattern of Glastonbury Abbey and Stonehenge. The full view of pristine Mt. Shasta looms ever-present, as are her Siberian Husky/wolves, who frolic just outside the studio window.

Her work has graced the covers of books, magazines, calendars, posters, cards and CDs in the US, Australia, and Europe, and can be seen in many private collections and museums.

With her paintings, Cheryl brings images from the higher dimensions into the field of time and space. Her highest aspiration is the infusion of Spirit into matter.

About the Author

Mother, artist, healer, and author, Christine Chalenor was born and raised in California. She makes her home in the pristine beauty of Mount Shasta. She has two sons, three daughters, three stepsons, and three granddaughters. She loves nature. You can find her hiking a trail, jumping into a cold alpine lake, cross country skiing through a snow covered meadow or tending her flowers, although providing a comfortable home for her family and friends is her priority.

Gifted at a young age with psychic abilities, she had many spiritual experiences which set her on the path to find answers. She would ask her mother to take her to different churches, so she could listen and learn from the varied religions. The knowledge and experience she gained set in motion a deep desire for truth. At age twenty-three she made seeking out truth her life's work.

Her quest led her through the studies of psychology, philosophy, religion and metaphysics. It also inspired travels through Europe and Egypt. In 1984 she shifted her focus to healing, studying accupressure, reflexology, and Reiki.

She became a Reiki Master in 1991. She has also worked for many years as an artist; her current medium is stained glass.

She is very optimistic about the future. These prayers reveal the depth of love and compassion she has for the planet and humanity. It is her faith and love for the Angels that has helped her through many difficult times.

This book is her gift to you. May you find the truth you too are seeking, and may the Angels—who are just a whisper away—light your path.

Contact and Ordering Info

Essene Teachings

Translated by Edmond Bordeaux Székely, *The Essene Gospel of Peace* has sold almost three million copies. Write for a complete list of available publications.

> The International Biogenic Society
> P.O. Box 849
> Nelson, BC
> CANADA V1L 6A5

Author Christine Chalenor

Fax: 530.926.5609
Email: angels@christinechalenor.com

Visionary Art by Cheryl Yambrach Rose

P.O. Box 919
Mount Shasta, CA 96067 USA
Phone: 530.926.6738
Fax: 530.926.6877
Email: cheryl@cherylrose.com
Website: www.cherylrose.com

Additional copies of Calling All Angels

$22.00 plus shipping ($3.50 US, $4 Canada, $7 foreign), California residents, please add sales tax.

Christine Chalenor
P.O. Box 905
Mt. Shasta, CA 96067 USA

Fax: 530.926.5609
Email: angels@christinechalenor.com

Website: www.christinechalenor.com